Progress of Doctrine

By Bob Mumford

LIFECHANGERS®

P.O. Box 3709 ❖ Cookeville, TN 38502
931.520.3730 ❖ lc@lifechangers.org

The Scripture quotations contained in this book are from:
    The New American Standard Bible®, Copyright ©
1960, 1962, 1963, 1971, 1972, 1973, 1975, 1977, 1995 by The
Lockman Foundation. The Amplified Bible. 1987. La Habra,
CA: The Lockman Foundation.

PLUMBLINE

Published by:

LIFECHANGERS ®
LIBRARY SERIES

P.O. Box 3709 | Cookeville, TN 38502
(800) 521-5676 | www.lifechangers.org

All Rights Reserved
ISBN 978-1-940054-17-9

© 2018 Lifechangers
All Rights Reserved
Printed in the United States of America

Progress of Doctrine

By Bob Mumford

I begin with a simple yet often disregarded idea that has become an important part of my personal journey. Jesus states it sort of off-handedly, like everyone should have known this. He says, "For whoever has, to him more shall be given" (Matthew 13:12). An examination of that statement will allow us to see and embrace a very important concept of spiritual growth. It goes something like this: There lay, hidden in plain sight, concepts of the Kingdom that will be opened to those whose hearts are seeking and pressing into the things of the Lord. Consider the privilege that Christ retains for Himself. Jesus says, "I have many more things to say to you, you cannot bear them now" (John 16:12). Time is Father's gift to the human race; it prevents everything from happening at once.

My intent in this Plumbline is to present ten aspects of what I would want to identify as Kingdom truths that will allow us to move from where we are to a more inclusive sense of identity and free embrace within the Kingdom.

I am seeking to establish the idea of our being more humanly responsible for what is identified as "pearl trading" (see Matthew 13:44-45). These ten things, if properly engaged, will bring life and progress. Our own growth process enables us to see into the issues more fully. When truth expands, it makes continual, fresh, and new application. As truth allows itself to be seen in a more mature manner, our prior understanding is not made to be error but becomes increasingly inadequate.

The principle behind my thesis can be understood and applied by explaining the idea of progress of doctrine. Progress of doctrine requires us to consider and embrace the obvious fact that various understandings of doctrine and models of evangelism, including the manner and method of our approach to Christ, have undergone a multitude of alterations and modifications. We would hardly recognize doctrine that was presented as normal prior to the time of Martin Luther. However, at that point in time, it was considered "normal."

What I seek to establish, is the startling fact that most ideas, concepts, and religious trends are only workable for a certain period of time and then pass into what used to be. These truths are not to be discarded, simply understood and applied differently. Biblical truth is a Person. The Person of Jesus has governmental purpose that causes particular emphasis on the earth to fluctuate, transition, and find new application in time. New and fresh insight requires us to trade our pearls.

The title for this Plumbline has been taken from an actual book. Thomas Bernard wrote *Progress of Doctrine* in Oxford, England, 1869. It is not easy reading. Understand I am not asking for you to read it, but it has served to shake me out of my limited and exclusive Pentecostal ideas that form the content of present truth and establish priority.

Here is how I would like for you to approach this Plumbline. My unqualified conviction and persuasion is: God the Father, by means of the Person of Christ and the work of the Holy Spirit, is preparing the entire world to see and understand that God is about to change the Kingdom delivery system in some drastic, unusual, and demanding way. Let's allow the following ten observations to lead us to embrace Truth's continual, fresh, and new application.

1. MOVING FROM TRANSACTIONAL TO RELATIONAL

Getting a grip on this first one will determine how and in what manner the other nine will bring life and freedom. The Old Testament is transactional. If you do this, I will do that, says the Lord. Moses Law is given in transactional motive. External obedience is the issue.

The New Testament is relational. The transactional can only take us so far. If we want to know Him and allow Him to know us, we must embrace the drastic change in the delivery system from the Old Testament to the New Testament and from transactional to relational. What we are all about to learn is that the relational is far more demanding and absolute.

Here is the basis for my statement: "But as many

as received Him, to them (the ones who seek to move toward Father's purpose) He gave the right to become children of God (relational authority to see and proclaim that they are now an active participant in Father's Own family) even those who believe on His Name" (John 1:12). All that has been transactional (Genesis to Malachi) has now been changed to that which depends upon our love for God and our maturity in learning how to respond to God with "all my heart, soul, mind and strength" (Matthew 22:37). Kingdom is now a love relationship between a Bridegroom and a bride. External sacrifice has become internal.

Tithing exemplifies the transactional. Giving has now been transformed into relational reality: now that I am God's family, He does not and will not extract the tithe. He begins to allow us to mature by learning to understand His redemptive act declares that all I am, all I think, all I own is now given to Father in relational response to Him as my Lord, God, and my Father. If we were to state it bluntly, 10% is nothing compared to His quiet and powerful expectation that watches how we give and invest our finances, time, and talent. Transactional tithe is one of the issues that hinder us from spiritual maturity, failing to reveal motive and corruption hidden in the folds of "paying our tithe."

When we raise the issue of tithe a thousand issues open, something like bailing the ocean with a teacup. It is amazing to see what things effectively prevent maturing in a relational Kingdom. Transactional tithing is a religious stronghold. A strong hold means that it is something in my mind that keeps me from knowing God. We are seeking to discover the changes in the delivery system. "The truth will set you free," meaning the presuppositions and the strong holds of our minds are removed (John 8:32).

If we continue to insist on making transactions with God: *if you will heal my mother, I'll read twenty chapters of Scripture every day,* we reveal our failure to understand that God ceased being a sheriff (transactional). God allowed Jesus to say: "Now My Father is a farmer" (John 15:1 Greek). He grows people in a relational matrix. We are now a bride to a Bridegroom whom He is preparing for Himself.

Our response must be childlike. Once we know this, we are going to cease trying to make transactional deals with God. God's pleasure and prosperity do not depend upon tithes but authenticity of our relational responsibility toward God and His Kingdom purpose. Cease to make vows that result in personal failure and consequent condemnation. Eagerly embrace the idea that God in Christ has inseminated you with Agape DNA and has given you authority to become part of his family.

A word of support for those who may disagree with me intensely! Please consider: I am not denigrating tithe. It is a most wonderful and effective, biblical insight. We are seeking to move everyone toward that maturity or perfection stated in Colossians 1:28.

2. KINGDOM AS A PRESENT REALITY

Nothing, in my estimation, has been more complex, injurious, and outright devastating as placing or forcing the Kingdom into the future. Embracing a future Kingdom gives us release from the sense of present obedience in time.

When we say "Our soon-coming King," we have already badly injured the intended purpose of the Kingdom as governing reality. If we say: "Our present loyalty and obedience is to Jesus Christ, whom we have embraced as our Lord and master in this present life," we are approaching reality. We deal with time and eternity in the present. A soon-coming King allows us to be quite free to do our own thing in His absence. The New Testament proper response to God as a Father is to ask: "How may I do your will on the earth as it is in Heaven?" (Matthew 6:10).

The Kingdom of Christ has been designed and intended to function in time. Luke 22:28-30 states that Jesus has been given a Kingdom, by the Father. He was given that Kingdom in time. He, in turn, imparts that Kingdom to His disciples in time. They have chosen to follow Him in time. Activity and purpose of the Kingdom has been destined to function in time. At the fullness of time, the responses and activities of the Kingdom of Christ revealed in time will be revealed in eternity. All of our actions, motives, and personal choices in time will affect the issues of eternity when God, as Father, receives Christ's Kingdom in time.

Then, by means of a given set of circumstance, God moves it into eternal dimension, allowing God to become all things to all people.

We must be able to see the concept of present Kingdom with new eyes and hear with spiritual ears as we look at the explanation that Paul carefully provides in 1 Corinthians 15. This is most critical. Please, for your own sake, go over this sequence, repeatedly, until you own it. I promise: you will need this very soon!

Then comes the end, (of time) when He hands over the kingdom (of Christ, that functions on earth in time, Mt. 6:10) to the God and Father, when He (Christ) has abolished all rule and all authority and power (He must accomplish this on the earth and in the time/space assignment). For He (Christ and His Kingdom agenda, which includes us) must reign (in time) until He has put all His enemies under His feet (on the earth and in time, Rom. 16:20 "the God of peace will soon crush Satan under your feet").

The last enemy that will be abolished is death (death is a weapon in time and then destroyed as stated clearly in Heb. 2:14).

For He has put all things in subjection under His feet. But when He says, "All things are put in subjection," it is evident that He (God as Father) is excepted who put all things in subjection to Him (Father gave Him the Kingdom in time, which He imparted to the 12 disciples in time; who imparted that Kingdom to us in time, all of this is repeated in Heb. 2).

When all things are subjected to Him (because Christ and His Kingdom agenda accomplished this in time), then the Son Himself (Who was given that Kingdom in time Luke 22:29) also will be subjected to the One who subjected all things to Him, so that God may be all in all (time ceases and the mystery of the Kingdom in time has been completed, Rev. 10:6&7, eternity begins, revealing the events, process, and responses on the earth; humanity is restored to God as a Father) (1 Cor. 15:24-28).

Jesus instructs us to "seek first the Kingdom" (Matthew 6:33). The Kingdom involves our personal transformation, our godly conduct, our responses, and our mindset in time. Proper response to the Kingdom in time prepares us for eternity. He is preparing us to be presented to the Father.

"Sell all you have and buy the field" (Matthew 13:44). Trade your pearls in time. If we don't do it in time, it does not and cannot happen in eternity! What we are looking at is the Kingdom intent to restore human responsibility that has been lost, refused, or denied in religious confusion. This is the restoration of the Kingdom delivery system.

Jesus imparted the Kingdom in time, and all of us are thinking and acting as if we are already in heaven. No. Heaven is coming to Earth, and the Kingdom, the New Jerusalem, is what Father is after in governmental reality in this life.

3. DIFFERENCE BETWEEN BEING WHOLLY WRONG AND INADEQUATE

Presuppositions often function as mental and emotional strong holds. These strong holds behave as mental blocks that keeps us from knowing the authentic Kingdom purpose of the God of the Bible. One day, looking for a particular book on the shelf, I was impacted by discovering some 18 different books of Romans. I was shocked and thought, "How could there possibly be 18 books on the book of Romans?" This would not include several other books on Romans included in complete sets of commentaries. Why are we utterly unable to write one book on Romans? Shock: Truth is a Person. Truth is living, moving, encountering. Truth is not a set of facts that we find ourselves desperate to defend. Scriptural truth is eternal, unending, and comprehensive. Suddenly, I saw it: all doctrine is inadequate.

It is simply not possible for me to tell you everything about God. God is bigger than; more than;

other than all that could possibly be stated. So when I'm all done writing, teaching, or talking, all that has been shared is essentially inadequate. We do not and have not been given the capacity to make any final statements. The solitary and final statement is the Person of Christ (see Heb. 1:1-3). Everything else will pass away!

We must cease beating people with the strength and conviction of our own doctrine. Observe the implications of Paul's insight: "When I was a child, I used to speak as a child" (1 Cor. 13:11). Not wrong, just inadequate.

My wife and I have a friend who had a precocious, brilliant daughter. She and her dad were in the backyard when a bird, sitting on the limb, flew straight down and started to eat. She said to her dad, "The birdie fell." Her dad said, "No, the birdie did not fall; the birdie flew." She said, "No, the birdie fell" because she had no capacity to understand the aerodynamics of a bird's ability to fly straight down. Neither could her dad expand upon what had actually happened. Much had occurred but both of them discovered themselves unable to communicate effectively. This concept is identified as our being inadequate. She wasn't wrong; the issue is child-like inadequacy.

Please, let us be more considerate of people. Refuse to traumatize others because of a doctrine that you hold so intensely, so strongly. Most of us have dismissed others over a particular doctrine that we no longer believe.

4. A WORKABLE DISTINCTION BETWEEN LOGOS AND RHEMA

God's Logos is the Pattern Son. He is God's Idea made incarnate; He is God's final speech (Heb. 1:1-3). The concept of a Pattern Son suggests that we can always be consciously aware of where and why God is taking us on this journey—predetermined to be conformed to the image of the Son.

The Greek word Logos (Strongs #3056) is used 339X in the New Testament. Logos has been made manifest: seen, understood, replicated, and embraced. Christ, as the Logos of God, is the unlimited, the mystery, and the essential center of all God the Father intends to do in this time/space universe. Nothing could be more important.

The Greek word Rhema *(Strong's #4387),* is only used 56X. Rhema suggests God is speaking in some audible or discernable manner, and we must learn to hear and obey. These two words are not used interchangeably. Each has its own sound or implication. Rhema is a breath, a spoken word, compared to the written word or Logos. Synergistic? Of course they are. God has provided an avenue to be able to speak to us in particular and very personal circumstances, Rhema. Logos is the foundational reality by which everything else is measured, including how and in what manner we can learn to know His voice.

Luke 1:37 says: "No spoken Rhema (not Logos) from God is impossible to be fulfilled." Luke 1:38 says:

"Let it be done unto me according to the Rhema (not Logos) which You have spoken." Mary is able to hear God give her clear instructions. These instructions are, of course, in accordance with the entire Logos of God, revealed in the Person of Christ. Maturity, as God the Father seeks to impart to the Body of Christ, must include our ability to hear the Voice of God. Christ Jesus is the Voice of God in His life, ministry, obedience, death and resurrection. However, like Mary, we will need to embrace, then implement the instructions of our Lord: "My sheep hear my Voice" (John 10:27).

God does speak to people. Many good leaders and whole denominations refuse to believe that this is a possibility. They seek to avoid the danger and the crazies that have been known when people say: God told me to do it! In spite of the danger, God still speaks, and Rhema is when God speaks.

Where did Joshua get his Logos bible verse, instructing him to march around Jericho 7X? He heard his instructions as a Rhema from the Living God. Allow us now to explore two more illustrations that have serious impact upon us as present day believers: "Man shall not live by bread alone, but by every Rhema that proceeds from the mouth of God" (Matthew 4:4). Rhema at this point includes Logos, but Christ is seeking to open us to God's instruction in maturity. The other illustration that is quite stunning to me is: "The words (Rhema, not Logos) that I have spoken to you are spirit and are life" (John 6:63).

There are 56 of these waiting for your discovery. Take the time to use your concordance and by use of Strongs #4387, begin to adventure out into the real world of being able to learn how to hear the voice of God in context and safety. It will strengthen your faith and increase your adventure.

5. EMBRACING JESUS AS TRUTH REVEALED: COGNITIVE AND METACOGNITIVE

At this point, I should like to have you in a room for several hours so that we could examine together the essential reason for the new birth. Often we have minimized it, almost trivialized it in comparison to its greater and intended Kingdom application.

The fruit of the new birth, John says, is to see and enter a Kingdom dimension. Father is inviting us as the direct result of our having made a personal choice to surrender our personal sovereignty to the Lord Jesus Christ. Why did we do that? What are the implications of us having done so?

When Father invites us into His Space, identified as the Kingdom of God, it requires Him to provide the needed equipment for us to be able to see, hear, and function within that space. God is Spirit. We are dead in trespass and sin. Our spiritual capacity has been battered to the point of death. The new birth is for the purpose of impartation of God's Agape: giving new life but also enabling us to know Him by revelation and illumination. He seeks to impart that which we are required to identify as entering a spiritual dimension. This is not natural. It is supernatural. It is introducing us to Truth as a Person, which is revealed meta-physically. Meta, a Greek preposition meaning beyond or more than, is linked with physical. We are being enabled to see, understand, and embrace Truth that is spiritual, more than natural, beyond natural, more than human cognition. The natural man cannot see the Kingdom of God; metaphysical enablement must be supplied. The Death and Resurrection of Jesus Christ has accomplished this. He not only forgives, but eagerly equips. He takes us from the human (cognitive thinking) to the spiritual realm identified as metacognitive or more than human thinking.

We can see the movement and intentionality of what the new birth seeks to accomplish.

First: Father is seeking the human spirit that dwells in us. We are lost, and He seeks to bring us to Himself by means of our reception of Jesus Christ. The end result of which is insemination with the spirit of Christ who loved and obeyed His Father (John 4:24).

Second: After the awakening, we have entered the metacognitive: God is Spirit; eager for us to know Him and for Him to know us (John 17:3 and 4:24). Persons and society move up into the Kingdom dimension by having been enabled and equipped. We enter and embrace the Kingdom as God's Own sphere. It is a change in government: "He has delivered us from the domain of darkness and transferred us to the kingdom of his beloved Son" (Col. 1:13).

Third: Our awakening consists of an impartation of Christ's incarnational Agape that causes eyes to see and ears to hear the metacognitive dimension. Now we can detect and interpret the Presence of the Holy Spirit, understand Scripture, and become available to God for His Own purpose in the earth. We have been prepared to know His Voice.

Fourth: Reception of the Person of Christ enables me to hear spirit language, see, and enter a governmental entity that is both spiritual and mystical!

6. DWELLING IN GOD'S PROVIDENCE AS COMPARED TO HIS SOVERIEGNTY

We now seek to make application of the five previous sections. God rules as sovereign. He is the King of the earth; it belongs to Him. He is Creator and there is none besides Him. What He has sought and what we must begin to enjoy is the change in the manner in which God has chosen to govern His Own People. All belongs to Him. However, some have chosen Him, and His response is to be and become a Father to them. Christ has made God our Father. Sovereignty yields to Christ. God seeks to alter the manner in which He is free to engage and relate to us.

Fatherhood should be understood as a change in governmental reality. He seeks to be and become a Father. When you pray: "Say, Our Father" (Matthew 6:9). This constitutes a direct and dramatic change in the manner in which He seeks to know us and for us to know Him. Providence is purely relational.

God seeks to modify His Own sovereignty by approaching us in providence: our sins and transgressions are not remembered. Here is our principle that must never be neglected or forgotten. Failure or refusal to embrace God as providential returns us to His governmental reality that is identified as sovereign. His Kingship is the default mode: "every knee shall bow and every tongue shall give praise to God" (Romans 14:11). He intends to do it in a providential manner; however, anyone and anything that does not yield to His sovereignty will experience His unbending rule. While in Scotland, we saw John Knox's home. Inscribed was: "God's Providence is my inheritance."

7. WORKING DIFFERENCE BETWEEN SOUL AND SPIRIT

When Mary, the mother of Jesus, exalts God in the magnificate, she makes a clear and workable distinction between the two aspects of soul and spirit. "My soul magnifies the Lord, and my (human) spirit has rejoiced in God my savior" (Luke 1:46-47).

Soul and spirit are two different entities. While I am determined not to get theological, we are seeking a working difference rather than a distinction in definition. Soul is a term that seeks to identify my mind, will, and emotions. We can live, almost entirely in the soulish realm. Strong soul wants its own way, lives in the emotions, and demonstrates the histrionics of one identified as soulish.

Spirit, in this instance, signifies the human spirit that is being moved upon by the Holy Spirit. My human spirit is that for which God, as a Father, seeks. Jesus says explicitly: "God is a spirit and those who worship Him must worship Him in spirit and truth" (John 4:24). James says it something like this: God eagerly desires the (human) spirit that he has placed within us (James 4:5).

Staying with our workable application requires us to say: only God by means of the Holy Spirit can "divide the human spirit from the human soul" (Hebrews 4:12). This division is the nature of one authentically becoming spiritual. The human spirit, by means of the Christ dwelling within, begins to strengthen and grow into maturity, a human spirit operating as God intended. The human spirit can be fed, nourished, responded to, and cultivated. Spiritual things for a spirit diet. Conversely, there is a soulish diet.

The primary reason for making this distinction is not complicated: God is Spirit. For me to know Him, I must be increasingly spirit. Father and I are one; not one person but one in purpose and intentionality. I must become less soulish and increasingly spiritual. We do so by relational response and not transactional strain.

Incrementally, the human spirit becomes Agape telos or mature. The human spirit is now governing the soul and the physical body. Soul and body are now yielding to my human spirit. Spirituality, as it is presented in the New Testament, is now being brought forth. Jesus' human spirit ruled His Person. He always yielded to the Holy Spirit in synergy and without internal resistance. It is not magic; it is a continual choice. Physical or body dominion leads to obsessive-compulsive behavior. Soulish dominion leads to petulance, anger, murmuring, and discontent. Neither is wholly pleasing to a Father who is Himself a spirit. My soul magnifies the Lord and my spirit rejoices in God my Savior!

8. AN EXPENSIVE DISTINCTION BETWEEN PUFFED UP AND BUILT UP

To my great surprise, the phrase "some of you are puffed up" is used some 6 times in the New Testament. Paul was so matter of fact when he opened this idea that is seemed to stun me. The actual difference between built up and puffed up is quite profound. The more I examine this, the more I can see forms of deep, personal deception. Self-deception is most complex, difficult to engage and difficult to rediscover our freedom.

Puffed up is due to a fleshly mind (see Col. 2:18 compared with 2:7). Let's bear down on the distinction:

Now concerning things sacrificed to idols, we know that we all have knowledge. Knowledge makes arrogant, but love edifies. If anyone sup-

poses that he knows anything, he has not yet known, as he ought to know; but if anyone loves God, he is known by Him (1 Corinthians 8:1–3).

A. We all have knowledge.

B. Some use knowledge in a wrong and injurious manner.

C. When we do that, it causes us to be puffed up or arrogant. Religious arrogance.

D. Agape does not do that. Agape moves on the authentic person.

E. Agape edifies or builds up, our human spirit is strengthened.

F. In religious arrogance, if you do not see this distinction, you are ignorant of the biblical model.

G. If you make Agape to be the issue, Love God and (surprise!) He will love you.

H. The relational is confirmed as compared to transactional.

9. UNDERSTANDING WHY THE KINGDOM IS REQUIRED TO BE WITHIN

We are, to the best of our ability, trying to preserve both the progressive nature and the sense of each of these becoming accumulative. The goal is personal freedom. "It was for freedom that Christ set us free" (Gal. 5:1). We are free from all that prevents us from running with patience the race that has been set before us. When we enter the Kingdom as the result of the new birth, many believers actually think there is a literal place, in heaven somewhere, that can be identified as the Kingdom of God. If there were such, I too would be eager to go there!

Entering God's realm, His sphere, His space, is a relational encounter. He pursues His own in order to return them to His governmental realm, His space. Water baptism (Mt. 28:19) serves as baptizing our own corruption, giving Father the de facto permission to transform our person. This permission is a consensual agreement for God to bring forth a personality transformation in us that emerges as one new man or one now conformed to the Image of the Son. He is, as amazing as it sounds, inviting us into relational integration with the Trinity as the Sweet Society.

We must consider the biblical reality that speaks of the New Jerusalem coming to earth. This signifies God's desire to see our human spirit governed now in the time/space earth (see Mt. 6:10). We surrender our personal sovereignty in this life as the result of our having embraced Christ and His Kingdom agenda. Re-examination of #2, will allow us to sort this out in our minds. No hidden agendas: Father wants you to know Him; He wants to know you. His Kingdom or ruling purpose has been placed within us, a spiritual reality that allows us to engage and become useful in a governmental sense.

Buying the field and trading our pearl must take place here on earth as we make our journey and tell our story. The Kingdom dimension is not a drill. It is ultimate reality and requests everything including heart, soul, mind, and strength.

Kingdom within involves the purpose and the people that have chosen to follow Christ and please the Father in a manner demonstrated by Christ as the Pattern Son. He is offering us something valuable and rather mind-blowing: If you will hear me knock, says Jesus, and open I will come in and we will sup and drink together. I will begin to open the mysteries of my own purpose like that encounter described on the Emmaus Road. "We knew Him in the breaking of bread" (Luke 24:35).

Kingdom within suggests: the effective termination of internal resistance; cessation of propensity to go my own way; becoming increasingly comfortable with God as my Father; learning His personal value system; presenting myself as a living sacrifice; seeking to know how to accomplish His will in the earth!

All of this should not and cannot be put off until the millennium. It does not and cannot wait until the physical coming of the Lord Jesus. His Kingdom purpose is what Jesus asks us to make priority in this life and on our journey. All that is in time effects and prepares us for all that is eternal.

10. EMBRACING AGAPE AS CONTAINING GOD'S ABSOLUTE

In 1984, in a tragic moment of my life the Lord Jesus, in what I consider to be one of the most significant rhema words of my journey, asked me for a very personal response. The question was not complicated: "Will you follow the biblical concept of Agape, knowing that I AM Agape, where ever it may take you?"

I was perfectly aware that this was not a drill. My answer would cost me and obedience would be greatly rewarding. It has been 34 wonderful years of an exciting and fulfilling encounter with the Life and governmental intention of the Father, Son, and Holy Spirit.

Agape in all of its forms is used some 320 times in Scripture. Scripture along with Church history affirm the following conviction: Agape is God's power, ruling force, and source of all His actions in the earth. Agape is the route to restoring the supernatural. Agape is the biblical absolute for which all humanity has searched!

About ten years ago, I discovered this theme in a marvelous exegetical book entitled: *Paul The Apostle*, by Romano Penna. To summarize these most impacting words: Luther was right. Faith works by Agape. If this is accurate, and we know it is, then the next reformation or Holy Spirit visitation will be identified by these words: Agape alone! Luther understood faith alone. We will be centered in Agape Alone. For the simple reason: faith works by Agape (Vol. I, Liturgical Press, Page 191f).

The larger Church is so sin conscious that it can paralyze us making us incapable of being Father conscious. Agape is relational. It is within: Agape serves to reveal God; It reveals Christ; It is manifest when the Holy Spirit is present. The solitary manner in which we can mature is by means of Agape being made mature within each, individual believer. It is Agape perfected that conforms us to the Image of God's Son: Christ replicated, for which all Creation waits (Rom. 8:19).

Recently I discovered a translation of sin or Greek hamartia. The author, with great care, declared the Greek would suggest hamartia as acting out of character. This was impacting for me. Every one of the other nine points is all enmeshed in this final point. I could prophesy the implications and the urgent necessity of our discovering and implementing a new and different delivery system, Agape. In closing I have included the following qualities of Agape taken from Brian Mclaren's *The Great Spiritual Migration*.

1. Agape is essential: without it, nothing else matters
2. Agape is patient
3. Agape is kind
4. Agape is generous, not envious
5. Agape is appreciative of others, not boastful of self
6. Agape is humble, not arrogant
7. Agape is courteous, not rude

8. Agape is flexible, it does not insist on its own way
9. Agape is gracious, not irritable
10. Agape is merciful, not resentful
11. Agape is positive, not rejoicing in wrongdoing; rejoices in truth.
12. Agape is resilient: bearing, believing, hoping, and enduring all things
13. Agape is perpetual: it never ends, never goes out of style
14. Agape is supreme, even greater than faith and hope

LIFECHANGERS ®

P.O. Box 3709 ❖ Cookeville, TN 38502
931.520.3730 ❖ lc@lifechangers.org

www.ingramcontent.com/pod-product-compliance
Lightning Source LLC
Chambersburg PA
CBHW060044040426
42331CB00032B/2427